U.S. Department of Justice
Civil Rights Division
Disability Rights Section

I0448751

Americans with Disabilities Act

ADA Guide for Small Towns

**A guide for small local governments
including towns, townships, and rural counties.**

Reproduction

Reproduction of this document is encouraged.

Additional copies of this publication may be obtained by calling the ADA Information Line at 800-514-0301 (voice), 800-514-0383 (TTY) or by visiting the Department's ADA Home Page on the World Wide Web (www.usdoj.gov/crt/ada/adahom1.htm).

Disclaimer

The ADA authorizes the Department of Justice to provide technical assistance to individuals and entities that have rights or responsibilities under the Act. This document provides informal guidance to assist you in understanding the ADA and the Department's regulation. However, this technical assistance does not constitute a legal interpretation of the statute.

first printing, April 2000

Table of Contents

Introduction

The Americans with Disabilities Act gives civil rights protections to individuals with disabilities similar to those provided to individuals on the basis of race, color, sex, national origin, age, and religion. It guarantees equal opportunity for individuals with disabilities in employment, transportation, State and local government services, telecommunications, and in the goods and services provided by businesses.

Small towns offer a variety of essential programs and services that are fundamental to the public and to everyday American life. Although the range of services offered by small towns varies, it is essential that people with disabilities have the opportunity to participate in the programs and services that towns offer. Applying for a building permit or business license, playing ball in the local park, marching in the Memorial Day parade, attending an annual street festival or a town meeting, or calling 9-1-1 for emergency police, fire, or rescue all are typical town programs, activities or services covered by the Americans with Disabilities Act or ADA.

The ADA gives people with disabilities an equal opportunity to participate in the mainstream of public life offered to all Americans. This guide presents an informal overview of some basic ADA requirements and provides cost-effective tips on how small towns can comply with the ADA.

Part One: The ADA's Requirements for Small Towns

Title II of the ADA applies to State and local governments, including towns and townships, school districts, water districts, special purpose districts, and other small local governments and instrumentalities. It prohibits discrimination on the basis of disability in all services, programs, and activities provided by towns[1]. Thus, people with disabilities must have an equal opportunity to participate in and benefit from a town's services, programs, and activities. To accomplish this, the ADA sets requirements for town facilities, new construction and alterations, communications with the public, and policies and procedures governing town programs, services, and activities.

A ramp located next to the stairs to this town hall provides an accessible entrance.

---

[1] The term "towns" is used in this publication to refer to all small local governments, towns, and townships. Please remember that title II applies to all State and local government entities, regardless of size, including State governments, local governments, special government entities such as transportation authorities, school districts, water districts, and other special purpose districts.

1. Existing Facilities: Program Accessibility

When programs, services, or activities are located in facilities that existed prior to January 26, 1992, the effective date of title II of the ADA, towns must make sure that they are also available to persons with disabilities, unless to do so would fundamentally alter a program, service, or activity or result in undue financial or administrative burdens (see page 8). This requirement is called program accessibility. When a service, program, or activity is located in a building that is not accessible, a small town can achieve program accessibility in several ways. It can:

- relocate the program or activity to an accessible facility,

- provide the activity, service, or benefit in another manner that meets ADA requirements, or

- make modifications to the building or facility itself to provide accessibility.

Thus, to achieve program accessibility, a small town need not make every existing facility accessible. It can relocate some programs to accessible facilities and modify other facilities, avoiding expensive physical modifications of all town facilities.

Example

A town holds its annual town meeting in an inaccessible location, the second floor of the two-story town hall that has no elevator. The town council considers installing an elevator in the building as well as replacing the existing town hall with a new, fully accessible building, but determines that the town's limited financial resources will not allow either of these approaches. Instead, the town officials decide to hold the town meetings, as well as other public meetings where large numbers of the public are expected to attend, in the accessible auditorium of its local high school. The town officials also decide to move smaller meetings, which are periodically held on the second floor of the town hall, to the school auditorium, when they receive a request within 24 hours of a meeting.

Example

The town library is a historic structure that is listed on the State historic register. The two entrances to the facility each have four steps and no accessible entrance is provided. The town consults with an architect to determine if an accessible entrance can be provided and is told that a ramp or lift cannot be added to either entrance without a significant change to the exterior of the building. After reviewing the ADA requirements, the town learns that qualified historic buildings and facilities are not required to take any action that would threaten or destroy the historic

Physical modifications to provide program accessibility included parking spaces, the public toilet facility and an accessible route to the ocean overlook.

Library staff provide curbside services because the library facility cannot be made accessible.

Example (continued)

significance of a historic property. The State historic preservation office is consulted and it determines that the exterior cannot be modified. Because physical modifications to the entrances cannot be made, the town changes its policies and provides access to the library services in an "alternate manner" upon request. Library staff are trained to take requests over the telephone, to look up information for individuals with disabilities who cannot use the library, to provide information over the telephone, and to provide curbside service for books and library publications or to mail items to individuals upon request. Library staff may also meet with an individual in another accessible location when the telephone service is not effective. The library publicizes a telephone number for requesting these alternate services in its publications and announcements.

Example

A town-operated two story historic house museum, which dates from 1885, provides exhibition and instructional programs for the public. The focus of the program is the exhibition of a typical 19th century Victorian house.

The self-evaluation determines that the house is not accessible. After considering the options for providing access to the programs and services, the town decides that it is not possible to move the museum programs to other accessible locations because the historic house itself is a critical part of the historic house program. The town develops plans to alter the facility to provide physical access to the first floor. These alterations are planned in compliance with the historic preservation requirements of the ADA Standards.

After reviewing the alterations with the State historic preservation office, the town determines that the second floor cannot be made accessible without threatening the unique features and historic significance of the house. Because the town must consider alternatives to structural changes in these instances, the town establishes a policy to locate all temporary programs on the first floor. In addition, the town documents the second floor spaces and content using video or other innovative solutions and provides an accessible viewing area on the first floor.

Example

The town's police station has one step at the public entrance and there is no accessible entrance available. After considering its options for providing program accessibility, the town decides to modify the facility to provide access rather than relocate the police programs or services. After review of the programs and services provided at the station, the town determines that the public entrance, lobby, and service counter need to be accessible to provide program accessibility. Therefore, alterations are limited to those items necessary to achieve program accessibility. In this case, it includes providing a van-accessible parking space in the parking lot, an accessible route from the parking space to the modified public entrance, and an accessible service counter inside the police station.

A town chose to alter its police station rather than move its programs and services to another accessible location.

When a town becomes aware that a program is not accessible and plans to alter a facility to provide access, it may be necessary to temporarily relocate a program, service, or activity to a temporary accessible location or to temporarily offer the service in an alternate manner.

This temporary solution assures that the service, program, or activity is accessible during the time the alterations are planned and being implemented.

Example

The public toilet facilities at the town recreation area are not accessible. After consideration of whether to modify the facilities or to relocate the programs held at the recreation area, the town decides to alter the toilet facilities and the walkway leading to them. While the fundraising is done, alterations planned, and the work completed, the town provides temporary portable toilet facilities that are accessible.

When choosing a method of providing program access, a public entity must give priority to the one that results in the most integrated setting appropriate to encourage interaction among all users, including individuals with disabilities. In addition, a town may offer additional activities or services so an individual with a disability can more fully participate in, or benefit from, a program, service, or activity. However, when such special activities or services are provided for people with disabilities, the town must permit a person with a disability to choose to participate in services, programs, or activities that are not different or separate.

Example

The local town pool provides a swimming program for people with disabilities that includes additional staff who provide individualized instruction. A person with a disability participates in the program. The person applies to attend group swimming lessons that are open to the public even though these lessons do not provide specialized instruction. The town must permit the individual with a disability to participate unless doing so would fundamentally alter the program.

Because program accessibility may be provided in an accessible part of a facility when the remainder of the facility is not accessible, the public must be informed of the location of accessible features. Signs should direct the public to the location of accessible elements and spaces, including the location of accessible parking, the accessible entrance to a facility, and accessible toilet rooms. In addition, a town may issue a brochure or pamphlet with a map indicating the town's accessible features.

Example

A town hall has two sets of public toilet rooms. One set has been altered and is accessible, and the other set is not accessible. The town installs signage at the inaccessible toilet rooms directing people to the accessible toilet rooms.

Sign at an inaccessible entrance provides directions to the nearest accessible entrance.

Towns making modifications to a building or facility to provide program accessibility must comply with the ADA Standards for Accessible Design (ADA Standards) or the Uniform Federal Accessibility Standards (UFAS).

Example

The town outdoor recreation area has a ball field, parking lot, and a building with public toilets. Town officials note that the parking lot does not have accessible parking spaces and the toilet facilities are not accessible. The town decides to provide accessible parking spaces in the part of the lot closest to the route to the ball field by restriping that section of the parking lot, installing signage designating the accessible parking spaces, and

4

Example (continued)
by making sure the accessible parking spaces are on an accessible route to the recreation area. The town also modifies the toilet facilities to make them accessible. All alterations are done in compliance with the ADA Standards and signs are provided to identify the accessible toilet facilities.

in the future the ADA Standards will become the only design standard under the ADA. Because ADA requirements for new construction and alterations do change from time to time, towns should become familiar with any new design and construction requirements before a project starts (see Resources for free information sources).

Alterations done to provide program accessibility must comply with the ADA Standards.

Public toilets at a park were built to comply with the new construction requirements of the ADA Standards.

2. New Construction and Alterations

New Construction

ADA requirements for new construction have been in effect since January 1992. New buildings and facilities must comply with the new construction provisions of the ADA Standards for Accessible Design (without the elevator exemption) or the Uniform Federal Accessibility Standards (UFAS). This requirement includes facilities that are open to the public and those that are for use by employees.

The ADA Standards for Accessible Design (ADA Standards) were first issued in 1991 and have been selected as the ADA design standard by many towns. Although towns now have the option to choose either the ADA Standards or the UFAS, it is likely that

Alterations and Additions

When a building or facility is renovated or altered or added to for any purpose, the alterations or additions must comply with the ADA Standards. In general, the alteration provisions are the same as the new construction requirements except that deviations are permitted when it is not technically feasible to comply. Additions are considered an alteration but the addition must follow the new construction requirements. When existing structural and other conditions make it impossible to meet all the alteration requirements of the ADA Standards, then they should be followed to the greatest extent possible.

Basic Requirements for Alterations:

- Any alteration that affects the usability of a building or facility must comply with the requirements of the ADA Standards unless technically infeasible to do so. Alterations can be as limited as the replacement of a fixture or element, such as a lavatory, toilet, or piece of door hardware.

- When an element is replaced, the new element must comply with the ADA Standards if the minimum requirements for accessibility under the ADA have not already been met.

Alterations to existing town buildings follow the alteration requirements of the ADA Standards.

- When a town alters an area of a facility that contains a primary function area, the town has an additional obligation. The town is also responsible for making the path of travel to the altered area (room or wing), as well as the toilet rooms, drinking fountains, and public telephones serving the altered area accessible. Primary function areas are those areas of a building that include the primary spaces for which the building was constructed (for example, offices or meeting areas in a town hall, locker rooms in an athletic facility, or classrooms in a school or training center). The amount of money the town must spend to provide an accessible path of travel is limited to 20% of the overall cost of the alterations. If the path of travel alterations can be done for less than the 20% limit, then only that expenditure is required. If all the required accessible features are already provided then no additional expenditure is needed.

- When a qualified historic facility is altered, an exception to the alteration requirements of the ADA Standards may be used if the alteration threatens to destroy the historic significance of the building or facility. In these situations, special provisions in the Standards may be used for the element or space that would be threatened. In almost all situations, accessible design can be used without significantly impairing the historic features of the facility.

- The ADA Standards have specific requirements for additions. Additions, which include an expansion, extension or increase of the gross floor area of a building or facility, are considered an alteration to a facility but the area that is added must comply with the new construction requirements. Each addition that affects or could affect the usability of an area containing a primary function area must meet the path of travel requirements (see above).

3. Maintenance of Accessible Features

Towns must maintain in operable working condition those features that are necessary to provide access to services, programs, and activities -- including elevators and lifts, curb ramps at intersections, accessible parking spaces, ramps to building or facility entrances, door hardware, and accessible toilet facilities. Isolated or temporary interruptions in service or access are permitted for maintenance or repairs.

Example

When weather conditions such as snow and ice limit or prevent access to services, programs, and activities, a town that houses programs in an accessible facility will have to maintain access to ensure that those programs are accessible. Maintenance of accessible features would include the removal of snow from accessible parking spaces, parking space access aisles, the accessible route to the accessible entrance, and accessible entrances. Although temporary interruptions in services due to bad weather are expected, alternate services should be provided if snow and ice cannot be cleared in a timely manner.

Clearing snow from accessible parking spaces and the accessible route may be essential to provide access to programs, services, or activities.

Example

A town building that was built before the ADA went into effect has a lift that provides access from inside the building to the library. The town must maintain the lift in working condition to assure that the public has access to the library programs. If the lift is out of order, repairs must be made in a timely fashion. Until the repairs are made, the town should provide alternate service for wheelchair users and others with disabilities who can no longer gain access to the library. These services may include retrieval of library materials by staff who will meet with an individual in an accessible location.

A lift provides access to the programs and services held in this town library. If the lift is out of service, alternate services are provided in an accessible location until the lift is repaired.

4. Effective Communication

Towns must take appropriate steps to ensure that communications with members of the public, job applicants, and participants with disabilities are as effective as communications with others unless it is an undue financial or administrative burden to do so or it would result in a fundamental alteration (see page 8) in the nature of its program or activity.

Achieving effective communication often requires that towns provide auxiliary aids and services. Examples of auxiliary aids and services include qualified sign language interpreters, assistive listening devices, open and closed captioning, notetakers, written materials, telephone handset devices, qualified readers, taped texts, audio recordings, Brailled materials, materials on computer disk, and large print materials.

A sign language interpreter is one type of auxiliary aid or service that may be requested.

Towns must provide appropriate auxiliary aids and services where they are necessary to achieve an equal opportunity to participate in, and enjoy the benefits of, a service, program, or activity conducted by or for the town. The town must give primary consideration to the type of auxiliary aid requested by a person with a disability. However, the town may provide a different type of aid if it can show that it is an effective means of communication.

Example

A town prepares to hold its annual town meeting in the high school gymnasium. A request is made through the meeting coordinator for real time captioning to be provided for a person who is deaf. Real time captioning displays the spoken content from a meeting or a speech on a large television screen as text. The town gives primary consideration to the request but after discussing alternatives for providing effective communication with the individual who made the request, the town learns that the

individual is fluent in American Sign Language (ASL). The town offers to provide a qualified ASL sign language interpreter for the town meeting because it has determined from discussions with the individual that the interpreter can provide effective communication.

Determination of an undue financial burden or a fundamental alteration can only be made by the head of the town government or his or her designee and must be accompanied by a written statement of the reasons for reaching that conclusion. The determination of an undue burden must be based on all resources available for use in the program, service, or activity. When it is not possible to provide a particular type of auxiliary aid to achieve effective communication due to an undue burden or fundamental alteration, the town must take any other action that would not result in such burdens or fundamental alteration, but would nevertheless ensure that individuals with disabilities receive the benefits and services of the program or activity.

If a town communicates with applicants and beneficiaries by telephone, it should ensure that an effective telecommunication system such as communication using the relay system or a TTY (or TDD) be used to communicate with individuals who are deaf, hard-of-hearing or who have speech disabilities. A TTY has a keyboard and visual display for non-verbal communication with another TTY user or a relay system operator. The relay system is provided in each State and permits telephone communication between voice handsets and individuals using a TTY.

A town can choose to provide a TTY without significant expense. Some towns have decided to install a portable TTY next to a public pay telephone and to anchor the portable unit to a shelf. Electrical connections are enclosed to protect against accidental disconnection of power.

Requirements for effective communications also apply to "telephone emergency services" that provide a basic emergency service, such as police, fire, and ambulance, that are provided by public safety agencies, including 9-1-1 (or, in some cases, seven-digit) systems. Direct, equal access must be provided to all services included in the system, including services such as emergency poison control information. Where direct access is provided to callers, direct access by TTY users means the telephone emergency service cannot use a relay system or transfer all TTY calls to one operator while other callers have access to all available operators (for more information, see the Department's publication, *Access for 9-1-1 and Telephone Emergency Services Under the Americans with Disabilities Act*).

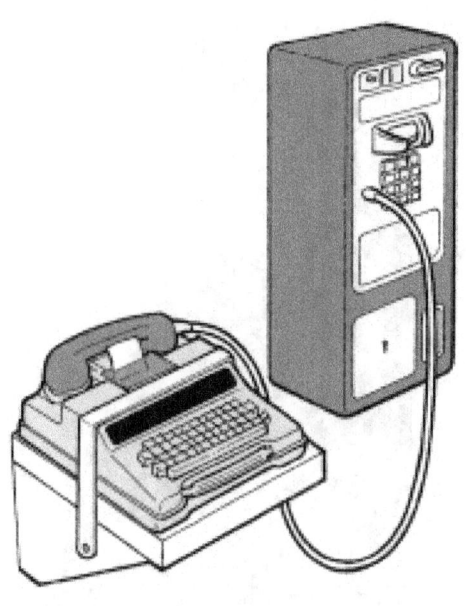

A portable TTY mounted on a shelf located next to a pay telephone can provide a low-cost TTY solution.

5. Policies, Practices, and Procedures

Towns must make reasonable modifications to policies, practices, and procedures to avoid discrimination against individuals with disabilities. While this requirement applies to all policies, practices, and procedures of the town, the town does not have to make modifications that would result in a fundamental alteration in the program, service, or activity or result in a direct threat to the health or safety of others. A direct threat is a significant risk that cannot be eliminated or reduced to an acceptable level by the town's modification of its policies, practices, or procedures, or by the provision of auxiliary aids or services. The public entity's determination that a person poses a direct threat to the health or safety of others may not be based on generalizations or stereotypes about the effects of a particular disability (see The ADA Title II Technical Assistance Manual).

The self-evaluation typically includes a review of polices, practices, and procedures (see page 10, Processes for Complying with the ADA). Periodic review after the self-evaluation may be done to maintain compliance with the ADA. A town can choose how it wants to conduct a review of policies and practices that govern the administration of the town's programs, activities, and services. Towns that have already done a self-evaluation do not have to do another one.

Review of policies, practices, and procedures also applies to telephone emergency services, such as 9-1-1, where policies must ensure direct access to individuals who use TTY's and computer modems.

A mother with her service animal leads her children to the town pool. Policies and procedures that restrict or prohibit service animals may violate the ADA.

Example

A town pool requires that adults provide photo identification to verify residency before using the pool or participating in pool programs. During review of town policies, practices, and procedures, the town determines that the pool identification policy, which requires that a driver's license with a photo be presented to gain admission, may discriminate against people with disabilities who may not have a driver's license. The town changes its policy to permit other forms of identification to verify residency.

6. Processes for Complying with the ADA

Towns that have not already conducted a self-evaluation or updated a previous self-evaluation conducted under Section 504 of the Rehabilitation Act must do so. The self-evaluation is a review of all town services, programs, and activities to identify any physical barriers or policies, practices, or procedures that may limit or exclude participation by people with disabilities. The self-evaluation includes permanent, temporary, and periodic services, programs, and activities. Each town should look at what services, programs, or activities are offered and in what location.

Any policies, practices, or procedures that may limit or exclude individuals with disabilities must be reasonably modified, unless doing so would result in a fundamental alteration in the nature of the service, program, or activity. The self-evaluation should identify changes to policies to be implemented. It should also identify any discriminatory policies, practices, and procedures that cannot be reasonably changed without resulting in a fundamental alteration.

The self-evaluation also identifies problems with the accessibility of facilities and establishes recommendations for providing program accessibility (which may include relocation to an accessible facility). It may also suggest short-term and long-term strategies to provide access to people with disabilities.

An emergency call box located in a rural area is mounted in an accessible location and can be used with or without speech to provide effective communication.

Towns that completed a self-evaluation to comply with section 504 of the Rehabilitation Act only have to bring the 504 self-evaluation up to date with ADA requirements by evaluating the services, programs, and activities that have changed. However, because considerable time has passed since most section 504 self-evaluations were done, it would be best to conduct a new self-evaluation.

Provide public notice about ADA requirements

A small town must provide notice to the public about its ADA obligations and about accessible facilities and services in the town. The notice must inform the public about the ADA's nondiscrimination requirements. It may also describe how the public or employees may contact specific town officials about problems with accessibility and the need for effective communication. The information must be accessible to the public, including people who have disabilities that affect communication, such as blindness, low vision, deafness, and hearing loss. Although no specific method is required to reach the public, notice can be provided in more than one format and by using more than one type of media, such as the town's website, print, radio, or television.

Other obligations for larger towns with 50 or more employees

Although the ADA only requires State and local governments with 50 or more employees to take the following measures, towns with less than fifty employees may want to consider following the same or similar steps because the process may make it easier to comply with the ADA.

a Designate an individual to coordinate ADA compliance

Responsibilities for the ADA coordinator may include conducting the self-evaluation and developing the transition plan (see below), handling requests for auxiliary aids and services, providing information about accessible programs and services, and serving as a local resource to the town or township. The ADA coordinator may also have responsibility for working with the mayor or town council to ensure that new facilities or alterations to town facilities meet ADA requirements. In some communities, this individual also receives complaints from the public and works to resolve them.

b Develop a transition plan

If a town with 50 or more employees decides to make physical changes to achieve program access it must develop a written plan that identifies the modifications that will be made. The plan should include timelines for completing these modifications. Interested parties, including people with disabilities and organizations representing people with disabilities, must at a minimum have an opportunity to participate in the development of the plan by submitting comments. A copy of the plan and a copy of the self-evaluation must be available for public inspection for three years after completion.

**Installation of curb ramps is one of the items included in the transition plan.
This type of curb ramp is used when some type of barrier prevents pedestrians from entering the curb ramp from the side.**

c Develop a grievance procedure

Towns with fifty or more employees must have an ADA grievance procedure. A grievance procedure provides people who feel they have been discriminated against because of their disability, or others who feel they have been discriminated against because they have a friend or family member with a disability, with a formal process to make their complaint known to the town. This procedure encourages prompt and equitable resolution of the problem at the local level without having to force individuals to file a Federal complaint or a lawsuit.

Part Two -- Typical Issues: Program Accessibility and Effective Communication

A Accessible Parking

In new construction and in alterations, accessible parking must be provided whenever public parking is provided. Towns may wish to add accessible parking when public parking is not provided to provide access to facilities where programs, services, or activities are located. Accessible parking spaces have a number of features that make it possible for people with disabilities to get into or out of a vehicle.

Accessible Parking Spaces for Cars

Accessible parking spaces for cars have at least a 60 inch-wide access aisle located adjacent to the designated parking space. The access aisle is just wide enough to permit a person using a wheelchair to enter or exit the car. These parking spaces must be located on level ground and identified with a sign mounted in front of the parking space high enough so it is visible when a vehicle is parked.

Features of Accessible Parking Spaces for Cars

Sign with the international symbol of accessibility mounted high enough so it can be seen while a vehicle is parked in the space.

If the accessible route is located in front of the space, install wheelstops or other barriers to keep vehicles from reducing width below 36 inches.

Access aisle of at least 60-inch width must be level (1:50 maximum slope in all directions), be the same length as the adjacent parking space(s) it serves and must connect to an accessible route to the building. Ramps must not extend into the access aisle.

Boundary of the access aisle must be marked. The end may be a squared or curved shape.

Two parking spaces may share an access aisle.

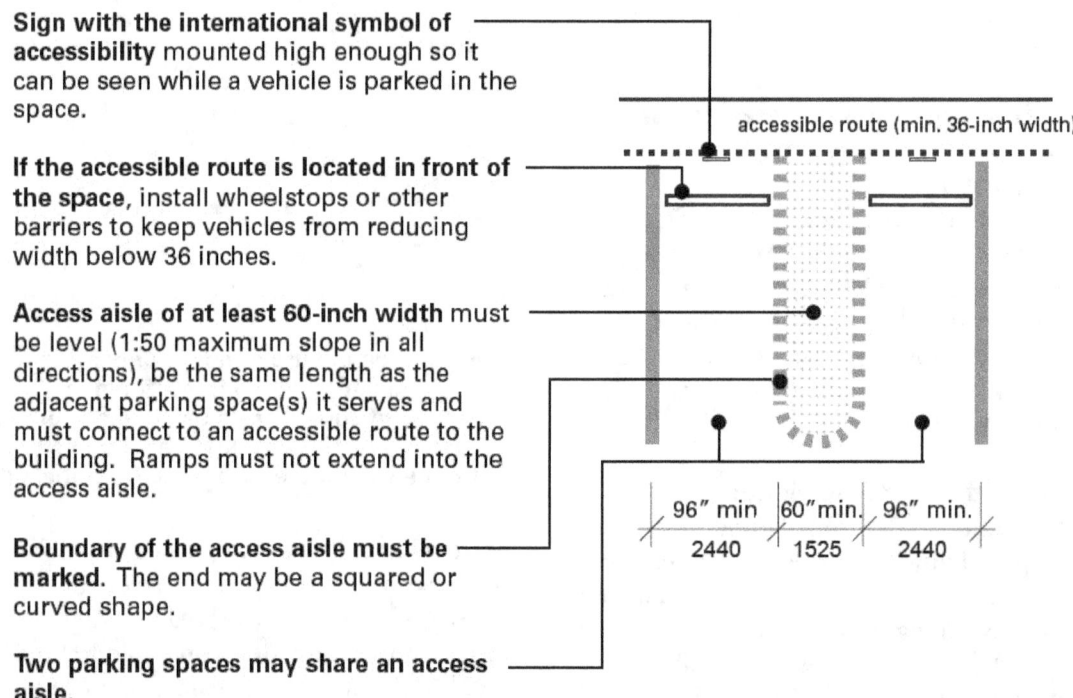

12

Van-Accessible Parking Spaces

One of every eight accessible parking spaces, but always at least one, must be accessible for vans with a side-mounted lift. If only one accessible space is provided, it must be a van-accessible space.

Van-accessible parking spaces incorporate the same requirements as accessible parking spaces for cars and have three additional features for vans:

- a wider access aisle (96 inch-wide) to accommodate a wheelchair lift;
- vertical clearance to accommodate van height at the van parking space, the adjacent access aisle, and on the vehicular route to and from the van-accessible space, and
- an additional sign that identifies the parking spaces as "van accessible."

When accessible parking spaces are added in an existing parking lot, towns must locate the accessible spaces on the most level ground close to the accessible entrance. An accessible route must always be provided from the accessible parking spaces to the accessible entrance.

The ADA Standards have technical requirements for parking lots and garages but no technical requirements for the design of on-street parking.

For more information about accessible parking, see the ADA Standards and other publications listed in Part III: Resources (page 20).

Three Additional Features for Van-Accessible Parking Spaces

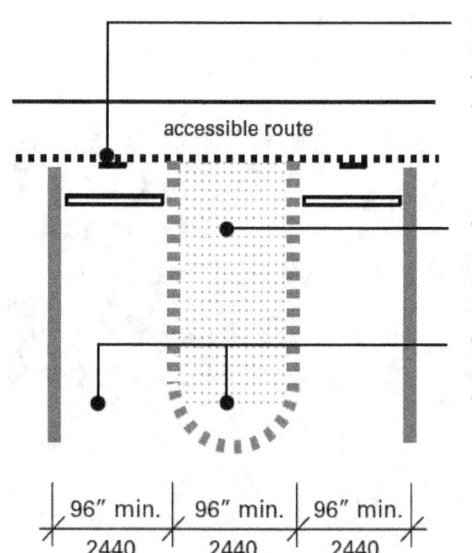

accessible route

96" min.
2440

96" min.
2440

96" min.
2440

Sign with "van accessible" and the international symbol of accessibility mounted high enough so the sign can be seen when a vehicle is parked in the space

96-inch min. width access aisle, level (max. slope 1:50 in all directions), located beside the van parking space

98-inch min. high clearance at van parking space, access aisle, and on vehicular route to and from van space

13

B Accessible Route

When a walk, pathway, or pedestrian route is necessary to provide public access to a program, service, or activity, an accessible route must be provided. An accessible route is an unobstructed pedestrian path that connects accessible elements and spaces such as accessible parking spaces, accessible entrances, accessible meeting rooms, accessible toilet rooms, etc. It can be a walkway, hallway, part of a courtyard, or other pedestrian space. An accessible route must be at least 36 inches wide, have no abrupt vertical changes in level (such as a step), have a running slope no more than 1:12 in most cases, and meet other requirements for cross slope, surface conditions, vertical height, and passing spaces. The width of an accessible route can be as narrow as 32 inches wide, such as at a doorway or a narrow section of hallway, but only for a distance up to 24 inches long.

An accessible route connects accessible parking (right) with the accessible entrance.

C Accessible Entrance

If entering a facility is necessary to participate in or benefit from a program, service, or activity, then that facility must have an accessible entrance and the accessible entrance must be on an accessible route. The accessible route must connect one or more (exterior) site entry points (such as parking, a public side-walk, or a public transportation stop) with an accessible entrance. The accessible entrance must also connect to an interior accessible route leading to the space or spaces where the program is located.

An accessible entrance must have an accessible door or doorway. If a door is provided, there must be maneuvering space on the pull and push sides of the door to permit a person using a wheelchair to open the door and then move through the door opening. The clear width of the opening must be at least 32 inches wide and accessible door hardware (handle and latch) must be provided. If a door closer is provided, it must be adjusted so the door will not close too quickly.

A historic town building added a ramp, walkway, and modified an entrance to provide access.

Although it is best to have the accessible entrance be the same one used by most of the public, existing conditions may prevent modification of the main entrance resulting in use of a secondary or side entrance as the accessible entrance. It may also be necessary to use a secondary entrance if only one part of the building is accessible. Where a secondary or side entrance provides access, signs should be provided at inaccessible entrances to direct the public to the nearest accessible entrance.

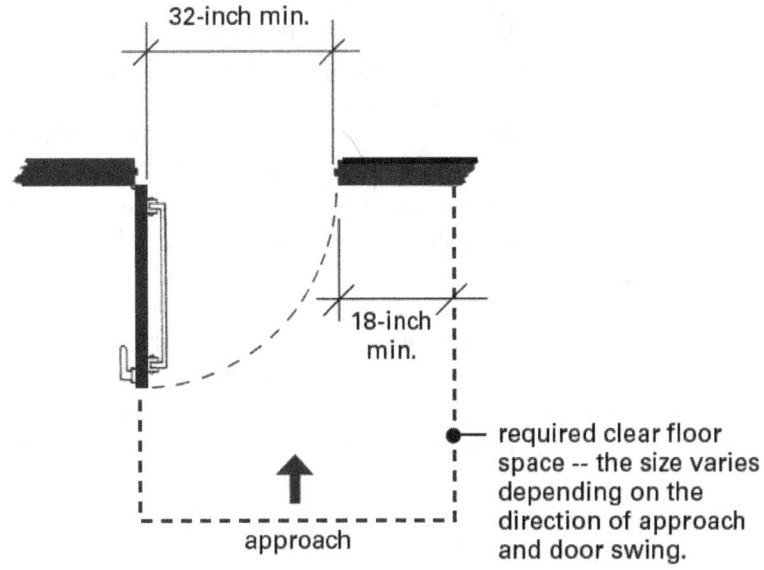

32-inch min.

18-inch min.

required clear floor space -- the size varies depending on the direction of approach and door swing.

approach

A plan view of an accessible door

D Curb Ramps at Intersections

Pedestrian walkways or sidewalks that are the responsibility of the town often play a key role in providing access to government programs and services and to the goods and services offered to the public by private businesses. When walkways cross a curb at intersections, a ramp or sloped surface is needed. The title II regulations set requirements for curb ramps at intersections. Whenever a town constructs a new road and sidewalk or alters existing roads and sidewalks, it must install curb ramps. In addition, the ADA requires that towns evaluate its existing system of sidewalks and develop a schedule to provide curb ramps where pedestrian walkways cross curbs. Because a town will not be able to install curb ramps at all town streets right away, the town's plan for curb ramp installation should set priorities for which streets require curb ramps. Towns must give priority to walkways serving State and local government offices and facilities, bus stops and transportation services, private businesses offering goods and services to the public, and employees, followed by walkways serving residential areas.

Curb ramps are needed when walkways cross a curb at an intersection. This type of curb ramp has flared sides and must be used when pedestrians may enter or exit the curb ramp from the side.

Any curb ramps that are installed must comply with the ADA Standards. In areas with hilly terrain or other site constraints, towns should follow the ADA Standards to the greatest extent feasible.

To achieve or maintain program accessibility, a town should develop procedures to allow the public to request that curb ramps be installed at specific intersections frequented by people with disabilities, including residents, employees, or visitors.

15

E Alternate Services

A town can make its services, programs, or activities accessible by relocating them to an accessible site or offering them in an alternate way that is accessible. A town should consider the integration requirements of the ADA, which require that priority be given to measures that will provide the service, program, or activity in the most integrated setting appropriate. For small towns, alternate service may include meeting with an individual with a disability in his or her home to fill out specific forms if the town office is not accessible. It may also include curb service to pick up or deliver an item. However, in some cases alternate service is not appropriate. If a town meeting is scheduled to be held on the second floor of a building without an elevator and a person using a wheelchair wishes to attend the meeting, the meeting should be relocated to an accessible space, unless it would result in undue financial or administrative burdens. Making the person sit by themselves on the first floor and watch the meeting on a television monitor or having them watch the meeting at home is not a desirable alternative because it does not give the person with a disability an equal opportunity to interact with officials and other participants.

F Library Services

Library services are an example of programs and services offered by many towns. If a library facility or building is not accessible, these services may be offered in a different accessible library facility, in another accessible facility nearby, or in an alternate manner. Some towns with only one library may prefer to modify the entrance to the library and other key elements to provide access. Others that may have a facility that is difficult to make accessible or lack the resources to make essential physical changes may choose to offer the programs and services in an alternate accessible location. What is important is that the same services be available to individuals with disabilities as are offered to others – such as doing research, using the card catalog or cataloging device, reading or reviewing items usually held in reserve or special collections, and returning loaned items.

An individual uses a call button to request assistance from library staff of the bookmobile.

If a library provides program accessibility through alternate means it must have policies that permit staff to carry out this policy. The policies must include procedures that permit the public to make requests for the alternate location or services. In many cases, however, providing basic physical accessibility to the library facility is preferred in meeting the obligation to provide services in the most integrated setting appropriate.

G Parks and Recreation Programs

A town's recreational programs or activities, such as those offered at the town baseball or football field or at the town pool, play an important part in the life of a community. These programs, services, and activities are among those that the town should review as part of the self-evaluation to determine if any physical or policy barriers exist that may keep people with disabilities from participating. If a town decides to modify facilities to provide program accessibility and has more than one facility available (such as when several ball fields are provided) only some of the facilities may need to be accessible. However, when only some of the ball fields are accessible, the scheduling policies for their use will need to accommodate requests for accessible fields, player areas, or spectator seating (if provided).

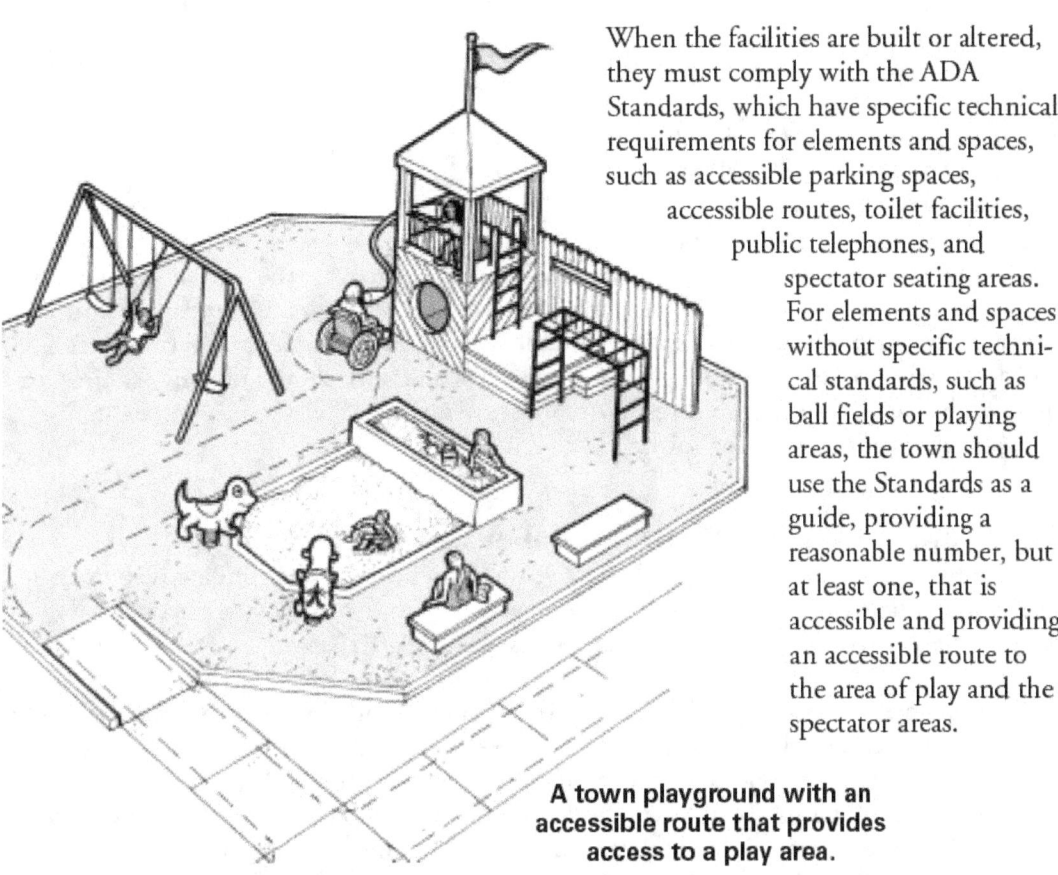

When the facilities are built or altered, they must comply with the ADA Standards, which have specific technical requirements for elements and spaces, such as accessible parking spaces, accessible routes, toilet facilities, public telephones, and spectator seating areas. For elements and spaces without specific technical standards, such as ball fields or playing areas, the town should use the Standards as a guide, providing a reasonable number, but at least one, that is accessible and providing an accessible route to the area of play and the spectator areas.

A town playground with an accessible route that provides access to a play area.

H Accessible Print Material

Public documents such as town annual reports, promotional brochures, and other documents, such as tax bills, license applications and other printed information may need to be provided in an alternate accessible format to provide effective communication for individuals who are blind or visually impaired. Alternate formats may include materials in Braille, large print, files on computer disk that can be used in a personal computer, or an audiotape recording of the print document. Priority should be given to the type of format that has been requested unless the town determines that another format is effective or that providing the one requested would result in undue financial or administrative burdens or a fundamental alteration in the nature of the program. A town should publish a contact number for the public to request an accessible format or other auxiliary aid or service.

▋ Police Services

Local police services are covered by the ADA, including investigations, interrogation, arrest, and transportation. Program accessibility requirements apply to the services and programs offered to the public, including those offered at a local police station. Effective communication requirements also apply to communication with the public, including individuals suspected of criminal activity.

A police officer and a deaf person communicate using a writing pad and pen.

If a town has a police station, jail, or holding facility, or other public police facility, the town should include services, programs, and activities that are offered in these facilities in its self-evaluation. To achieve program accessibility, it may be possible to share some accessible facilities with other nearby towns or government entities or to offer the service, program, or activity in another accessible location or manner. Vehicles used to transport suspects or prisoners should also be included in the self-evaluation. If a town does not have an accessible vehicle available for transporting suspects or prisoners, the town should identify a source for an accessible vehicle, such as an accessible school bus, taxi with a wheelchair lift, or an accessible vehicle from a nearby town.

▋ Calling 9-1-1 and Other Emergency Services

Dialing 9-1-1 is the most familiar and effective way Americans have of finding help in an emergency. The ADA requires all telephone emergency services to provide direct, equal access to their services for people with disabilities who use a TTY.

Equal access means that TTY callers have an opportunity to obtain emergency services that is equal to that of callers who use voice handsets. The telephone emergency services provided for TTY callers must be handled in the same manner as those provided for individuals who make voice calls, in terms of response time, response quality, hours of operation, and all other features offered (e.g., automatic number identification, automatic location identification, automatic call distribution). There must be adequate numbers of TTY's or equipment to answer TTY calls. If a town or township relies on another government entity to provide its 9-1-1 and telephone emergency services, it should inquire about the accessibility of the services (for more information see *Access for 9-1-1 and Telephone Emergency Services Under the Americans with Disabilities Act*).

▋ Temporary Events

The ADA applies to both temporary and permanent services, programs, or activities of a town. Facilities and structures that are built or altered for temporary use must comply with the ADA Standards (except for construction trailers). In addition, the policies and operations for the event must meet the nondiscrimination requirements of the ADA. When planning temporary events such as a town festival or concert, the town should review ADA title II requirements[2] and the ADA Standards. The Standards can provide guidance to help event planners place temporary accessible parking spaces in appropriate locations, provide an accessible route throughout the site, and provide other accessible features for food service, toilet facilities (including accessible portable toilets), assembly area seating, public telephones, etc., where such elements or facilities are provided for the public. It is very important to consider accessibility requirements when the event is in the planning stage so that accessible facilities can be identified and incorporated in a manner that does not require extensive construction or last-minute modifications.

Selected Accessible Features of Town Fair

- temporary curb ramp added where needed to provide an accessible route

- booths and vendors located on an accessible route

- sign language interpreters available for selected performances and programs

- accessible parking, accessible transit drop offs and stops (if provided) and an accessible route from these areas to the fair is provided

A town fair that was planned to provide accessible programs, services and activities.

Effective communication requirements also apply to temporary events. It may be necessary to provide qualified sign language interpreters or other auxiliary aids and services as requested, such as print material in a large-print format or on computer disk. A town may choose when to provide interpreters and publicize a schedule for interpreters and other auxiliary aids and services. It should also provide auxiliary aids or services in response to individual requests, unless to do so would result in undue financial and administrative burdens. Promotional material for a temporary event should explain how the public can request a particular auxiliary aid or service and be informed of when specific auxiliary aids and services may be available.

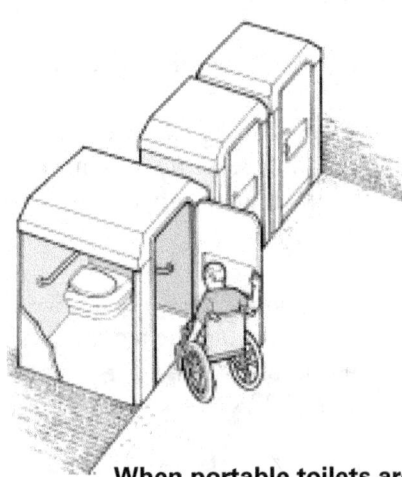

When portable toilets are provided, at least one at each location must be accessible.

---

[2] Private vendors and contractors should follow the ADA title III regulations which cover goods and services provided by private companies. For more information, see the *ADA Guide for Small Businesses.*

Part Three: Resources

Department of Justice ADA Information

To help State and local governments, including small local governments, understand and comply with the law, the Department of Justice established a technical assistance program to answer questions about the ADA. The Department of Justice has a toll-free ADA Information Line that provides access to ADA specialists during business hours. The ADA Information Line also provides twenty-four hours a day access to a fax-on-demand system for technical assistance materials that permits a caller to have the document sent to them by fax. Orders for publications sent by mail may be made twenty-four hours a day on the Information Line's voice mail system.

ADA Information Line -- **800-514-0301 voice** and **800-514-0383 TTY**

Another important source of ADA information is the Department's ADA Home Page on the World Wide Web. This extensive web site provides access to ADA regulations, all Department ADA technical assistance materials, including newly-released technical assistance material, proposed changes in the ADA regulations, and access to Freedom of Information Act materials including technical assistance letters. The web site also provides links to other Federal agencies with ADA responsibilities.

ADA Home Page -- **www.usdoj.gov/crt/ada/adahom1.htm**

Selected ADA Publications available from the ADA Information Line and ADA Home Page:

The ADA and City Governments:
Common Problems
A 9-page publication that compiles common problems with Title II compliance.

ADA Regulation for Title II, as printed in the Federal Register (7/26/91)
The Department of Justice's regulation implementing title II, subtitle A, of the ADA, which prohibits discrimination on the basis of disability in the services, programs, and activities provided by towns.

Title II Technical Assistance Manual (1993) and Supplements (Spanish edition available by mail)
A 30-page manual explaining what State and local governments must do to ensure that their services, programs, and activities are provided to the public in a non-discriminatory manner. Gives practical examples.

Department of Justice ADA Mediation Program
A 8-page publication describing the Department's ADA mediation program including locations of ADA mediators, and examples of successful mediation efforts.

ADA Regulation for Title III, including the **ADA Standards for Accessible Design.**

ADA Information Services
A 2-page list with the telephone numbers and Internet addresses of Federal agencies and other organizations that provide information and technical assistance to the public about the ADA.

Enforcing the ADA: A Status Report from the Department of Justice
A quarterly report providing timely information about ADA cases and settlements, building codes that meet ADA accessibility standards, and ADA technical assistance activities.

Commonly Asked Questions About the ADA and Law Enforcement
A 13-page publication explaining ADA requirements for ensuring that people with disabilities receive the same law enforcement services and protections.

Access for 9-1-1 and Telephone Emergency Services
A 10-page publication explaining the requirements for direct, equal access to 9-1-1 for persons who use teletypewriters (TTYs).

ADA Guide for Small Businesses
A 15-page booklet for businesses that provide goods and services to the public.

Other Federal Agencies and Federal Grantees Providing Information

Department of Transportation

Department of Transportation offers technical assistance on ADA provisions applying to public transportation.

ADA Assistance Line for information, questions and complaints
888-446-4511 (voice) -- TTY: relay service
202-366-2285 (voice) -- 202-366-0153 (TTY)

Transportation - documents and questions
202-366-1656 (voice) -- TTY: use relay service

Transportation - legal questions
202-366-4011 (voice) -- TTY: use relay service

Internet address -- www.fta.dot.gov

Equal Employment Opportunity Commission

Equal Employment Opportunity Commission offers technical assistance on the ADA provisions applying to employment; also provides information on how to file ADA complaints.

Employment - questions
800-669-4000 (voice) -- 800-669-6820 (TTY)

Employment - documents
800-669-3362 (voice) -- 800-800-3302 (TTY)

Internet address -- www.eeoc.gov

Access Board

Access Board (or Architectural and Transportation Barriers Compliance Board) offers technical assistance on the ADA Accessibility Guidelines.

Documents and questions
800-872-2253 (voice) -- 800-993-2822 (TTY)

Electronic bulletin board -- 202-272-5448

Internet address -- www.access-board.gov

Department of Housing and Urban Development

Fair Housing Act: for questions or publications call Department of Housing and Urban Development.

Fair Housing accessibility questions
202-708-2333 (voice) -- 202-708-4112 (TTY)

Fair Housing publications
800-767-7468 (voice) -- TTY: use relay service

Internet address -- www.hud.gov

Disability and Business Technical Assistance Centers (DBTACs)

Department of Education funds ten regional centers to provide technical assistance on the ADA.

800-949-4232 (voice/TTY)

Internet address -- www.adata.org

Job Accommodation Network

The Job Accommodation Network (JAN) is a free telephone consulting service offering information and advice to employers and people with disabilities on reasonable accommodation in the workplace.

800-526-7234 (voice &TTY)

Internet address --
http://janweb.icdi.wvu.edu/english